WHY A DAUGHTER NEEDS A MOM

100 reasons

GREGORY E. LANG

Cumberland House
Nashville, Tennessee

Published by
    Cumberland House Publishing, Inc.
    431 Harding Industrial Drive
    Nashville, TN 37211

Cover design: Unlikely Suburban Design
Text design: Lisa Taylor
Cover photo: Gregory E. Lang

Library of Congress Cataloging-in-Publication Data

Lang, Gregory E., 1960–
    Why a daughter needs a mom : 100 reasons / Gregory E. Lang.
       p. cm.
    ISBN 1-58182-380-0 (hardcover)
    1. Mothers and daughters–Miscellanea. 1. Title.
       HQ755.85.L338 2004
       306.874'3—dc22

                                                                    2003025382

Printed in the United States of America
2 3 4 5 6 7 8 — 09 08 07 06 05 04

To Becky—thank you.

INTRODUCTION

My daughter, Meagan Katherine, and I share a close relationship, albeit one that has changed remarkably since she has matured into a young teenager. Once my constant companion, my playful partner in crime, my most adoring audience, my child has become less enchanted with me as she has entered the initial phases of becoming a woman. Gone are the days of holding hands in public, kissing on the lips, and waking up to find that she had slipped beneath my bedcovers sometime during the night. These treasured gestures of affection are now replaced with brief and discrete touches, small talk, her need for privacy, and the occasional impatient admonishment: "Dad, I am *not* a little girl anymore."

I struggle with feelings of loss, and at times I cannot resist the impulse to implore my daughter to confide in me, to tell me what thoughts occupy her mind and what feelings beat in her heart. When she doesn't, I hang my head and worry that something has happened to us, convinced that we will never again be as close as we once were. Sometimes I fret that I cannot identify what my child needs or understand why she acts as she does. These thoughts occur to me when I am alone and my judgment is clouded by my sorrow. Thank God for moments of clarity, when I reassure myself that these changes aren't so perplexing after all, that they are, in fact, what should be expected and what should be supported, if indeed I intend for my child to become the strong, independent woman I hope for. It is then that I accept without reluctance that a dad cannot be *everything* to his daughter. It is then that I see so clearly that she needs her mother, too.

Becky, my ex-wife, and I have been divorced nearly ten years, and we share joint custody of our only child. Meagan lives for a time with me, and then her mom, and back to me. Becky and I live only a few miles apart. We have keys to each other's home, we talk on the telephone often, share meals together now and then, negotiate agreements about enforcing household rules or extending new privileges, resolve disputes about what we might do differently in our relationship with Meagan, and help each other in her care. Long ago we agreed that though we had resigned ourselves to becoming ex-spouses, we would *never* become ex-parents. It is as parents that our partnership lives on, and it is as parents that we overcome our issues with each other to find a way to do what is best for Meagan. It is in that role, as my partner in parenting, that Becky has been most valuable to me, especially as I learn to accept that my daughter is, most certainly, not a little girl anymore.

As my relationship with Meagan has changed, so too has her relationship with her mother. Now her most trusted confidante, Meagan enjoys lengthy and enthusiastic telephone conversations with her mother, discussing boys, girlfriend spats, celebrity news, or the latest reality television show. Now her fashion consultant, Meagan and her mom shop for hours, get their hair and nails done, and agree that when a girl packs her bags, she must include an abundant selection of shoes, "just in case." Now her preferred safe harbor, Meagan turns to her mother for consolation, protection, and understanding. As a woman, it is Becky who can comprehend what I cannot. As a mom, it is Becky who can give what I cannot. I admit that I occasionally look upon their relationship with a twinge of jealousy, but also always with deep joy and satisfaction that it is what it has become. Their relationship is not only good for them, but for me as well. It is after a late-night telephone call from Becky, explaining to me what I could not see or comforting me about some parental insecurity, that I am thankful she is the mother of my child.

A daughter needs a mom for many reasons, and by the very nature of the differences between men and women, some of these reasons may never be clear to me, but that does not negate their vital importance in a girl's life. Daughters need moms to help them understand what is happening to their bodies, to teach them how to make sound decisions regarding boys, to show them how to care for themselves, how to care for their children, and how to care for their marriage. Daughters need moms because they understand that sometimes tears come for no reason, that bad moods may simply mean nothing at all, that chocolate is a necessity, that being silly is fun, and that everything does not have to be practical or in accordance with a schedule. Daughters need moms because dads cannot be everything for them. Daughters need moms to help them grow into the wonderful women they have the potential of becoming.

I am not a mother, nor am I a daughter, and therefore in the minds of some perhaps ill-equipped to write this book. However, I am an astute observer of human relationships, and I am a member of a family. My family, comprised of a dad, a mother, and a child, is not unlike many, if not most, other families. It includes laughter and tears, hugs and arguments, surprises and disappointments, giving and taking, sacrifices and rewards. Although she lives in two houses, Meagan still has one family because her mother and I parent her together, love her together, and compromise with each other on her behalf. It is in gratitude to Becky for helping me give Meagan a sense of family that I wrote this book. I hope the story of our family will stir other ex-spouses to rally around their children and embrace the role they share as parents, and in doing so, give their children a more complete family experience, even if in two homes. With this book I hope to give other daughters and moms cause for celebrating what is unique and special about their relationship. I hope, too, to reassure Meagan that I understand, accept, and encourage her as she grows into a woman and reaches beyond me for what she needs. And finally, with this book, I say to Becky, thank you. Thank you for giving me such a wonderful gift, our child. Thank you for being such a great mom, giving to Meagan what I cannot. And thank you for continuing as my partner and giving me friendship when I need it most.

WHY A DAUGHTER NEEDS A MOM

A DAUGHTER NEEDS A MOM

to provide her with memories
that will last forever.

～∽⧫∾～

A DAUGHTER NEEDS A MOM

who is never more than a phone call away.

A DAUGHTER NEEDS A MOM

because no one understands girls like a mom.

A DAUGHTER NEEDS A MOM . . .

to help her interpret the language of boys.

to tell about her first kiss.

to teach her that class never goes out of style.

to flash the front porch lights when it is time
to come inside.

A DAUGHTER NEEDS A MOM

to tell her that beauty never fades
if you look in the right places.

A DAUGHTER NEEDS A MOM

who believes it is okay to see things differently.

A DAUGHTER NEEDS A MOM . . .

to remind her to say nice things when she talks to herself.

to teach her to love her friends, no matter what they do.

to give her the courage to stand up for herself.

to teach her that when nothing seems right,
do something normal.

A DAUGHTER NEEDS A MOM

to teach her how to cook.

A DAUGHTER NEEDS A MOM

who knows how to let loose and have fun.

A DAUGHTER NEEDS A MOM . . .

to teach her the art of conversation.

to teach her how to be a lady.

to tell her not to be afraid to seize the moment.

to point out that there is a difference between
being adventurous and being wild.

A DAUGHTER NEEDS A MOM

who can play on her level.

～✑～

A DAUGHTER NEEDS A MOM

because there are some things a dad
just can't handle.

∽☙∾

A DAUGHTER NEEDS A MOM

to read to her.

A DAUGHTER NEEDS A MOM

to show her how to give back to others.

A DAUGHTER NEEDS A MOM

to help her on her wedding day.

～⌒～

A DAUGHTER NEEDS A MOM

to catch her if she falls.

∾◎◠

A DAUGHTER NEEDS A MOM . . .

to soothe the pain of a broken heart.

to prepare her for what she will face when she leaves home.

to teach her that sometimes choosing to wait is a good idea.

to teach her that you cannot make someone love you,
but you can be someone who can be loved.

A DAUGHTER NEEDS A MOM

to remind her to be playful, no matter how old she is.

A DAUGHTER NEEDS A MOM

to remind her, on the bad days, that she is not alone.

A DAUGHTER NEEDS A MOM

to protect her from strangers.

~∞~

A DAUGHTER NEEDS A MOM

to remind her to save some time
and energy for herself.

~♧~

A DAUGHTER NEEDS A MOM . . .

to carry her when she is tired.

to show her the comfort of a warm embrace.

to sing her to sleep.

to teach her to laugh at herself.

A DAUGHTER NEEDS A MOM

to help her choose a prom dress.

A DAUGHTER NEEDS A MOM

who shares with her the wisdom of generations.

∼⌒∽

A DAUGHTER NEEDS A MOM

to encourage her to be whatever she wants to be.

A DAUGHTER NEEDS A MOM . . .

to teach her that even true love requires compromise.

to tell her what she should expect from a good man.

to prepare her for becoming a wife.

to show her how to raise a family.

A DAUGHTER NEEDS A MOM

to show her how to love someone with all her heart.

A DAUGHTER NEEDS A MOM

to explain to her how to set limits with boys.

A DAUGHTER NEEDS A MOM . . .

to show her how to use humor to lighten heavy loads.

to show her how to put a little love in everything she does.

to tell her not to let pride get in the way
of forgiving someone.

to encourage her to be grateful.

A DAUGHTER NEEDS A MOM

to help her see that death is a part of life.

～oo～

A DAUGHTER NEEDS A MOM

to teach her how to look her best.

～♋～

A DAUGHTER NEEDS A MOM

to teach her not to wait until tomorrow
to say, "I'm sorry."

A DAUGHTER NEEDS A MOM . . .

to help her learn how to color inside the lines.

to show her how to make use of what she already has.

to make sure she always receives mail.

to tell her that it is okay to be a tomboy.

A DAUGHTER NEEDS A MOM

to teach her to make thankfulness a habit.

A DAUGHTER NEEDS A MOM

to teach her that every tree takes
a while to grow.

～〇～

A DAUGHTER NEEDS A MOM

to encourage her to laugh as often as possible.

~⊙~

A DAUGHTER NEEDS A MOM

to give her the freedom to express herself.

~Ⓢ~

A DAUGHTER NEEDS A MOM

who knows how to put a smile on her face.

A DAUGHTER NEEDS A MOM

to listen closely to what troubles her.

A DAUGHTER NEEDS A MOM . . .

to share in her excitement when she falls in love
for the first time.

to share her daydreams with her.

who wants to help make her wishes come true.

to love her for who she is.

A DAUGHTER NEEDS A MOM

to teach her that she should know herself better
than anyone else does.

A DAUGHTER NEEDS A MOM

to nurture her imagination.

A DAUGHTER NEEDS A MOM

to show her that enthusiasm for life is contagious.

A DAUGHTER NEEDS A MOM . . .

to teach her that the path taken means as much
as the destination.

to teach her that her body is a temple.

to help her distinguish the difference between love and lust.

to remind her that there is a rainbow after every storm.

A DAUGHTER NEEDS A MOM

to indulge her individuality.

A DAUGHTER NEEDS A MOM

to teach her that she is responsible
for her own happiness.

~෧~

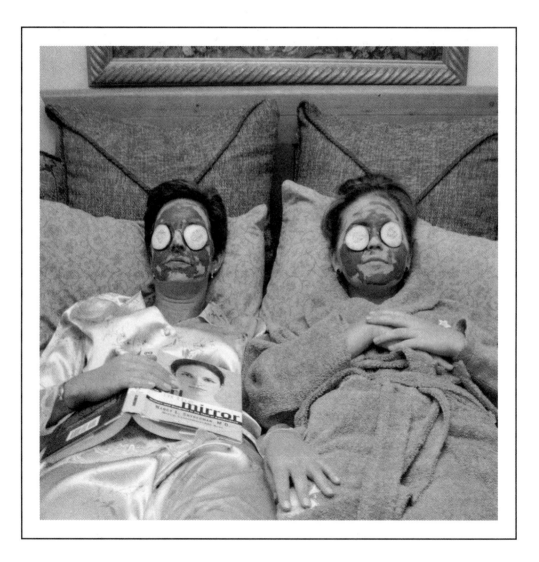

A DAUGHTER NEEDS A MOM

to remind her that she has the right
to indulge herself now and then.

A DAUGHTER NEEDS A MOM . . .

to tell her that the road to happiness is not always straight.

to explain that the sweetest flower may not
always be the prettiest.

to instill patience in her.

who never grows tired of holding hands.

A DAUGHTER NEEDS A MOM

who can read the expression on her face.

A DAUGHTER NEEDS A MOM . . .

who never hesitates to show affection.

who will sing along with her when her favorite
song comes on the radio.

who does not lose her identity in the role of wife and mother.

who shows by example that community
involvement is a worthy pursuit.

A DAUGHTER NEEDS A MOM

to teach her how to care for children.

A DAUGHTER NEEDS A MOM

to teach her that you cannot start a life over,
but you can change the way it ends.

～❧～

A DAUGHTER NEEDS A MOM

to teach her to lift her voice in praise.

A DAUGHTER NEEDS A MOM . . .

to show her how to fix her hair.

to tell her that grudges are too burdensome to carry.

to remind her that in faith there is fellowship.

to assure her that she always has a place
to come home to.

A DAUGHTER NEEDS A MOM

to teach her that women are not bound to the home.

A DAUGHTER NEEDS A MOM . . .

to make sure she keeps a true heart.

to comfort her through her tears.

to challenge her to strive for what is just beyond her reach.

who tells her of the special place
she holds in her heart.

A DAUGHTER NEEDS A MOM

to teach her not to let a good day
slip from her fingers.

A DAUGHTER NEEDS A MOM

because without her she will have less in her life
than she deserves.

～◎～

Acknowledgments

This book could not have been written without the support and generosity of many people. I offer a special thanks to the daughters and moms who shared their stories with me, who became my friends during this process, and who helped me find the heart of the matter, the profound and nearly endless reasons why daughters need their moms. I was deeply touched by the love I witnessed in the time I spent with you.

I also wish to thank my daughter, Meagan Katherine, and her friend Lauren Heusel, who helped me make sure this book had the right "girl touch," and the administration of Greater Atlanta Christian School, which helped me once more recruit families to participate in creating this book.

Finally, I wish to thank Ron Pitkin and the staff at Cumberland House, but especially my editor, Lisa Taylor. Lisa, in this fifth book we have completed together, I can truly say that you have added style to the books and made them better than I envisioned. May all my editors be so pleasant to work with. You have my deepest appreciation and warmest regards.

To Contact the Author

write in care of the publisher:
Cumberland House Publishing
431 Harding Industrial Drive
Nashville, TN 37211

or email:
greg.lang@mindspring.com